CONTENTS

FROM THE EDITOR

This month, we are honoring several powerful women entrepreneurs.

Dr. Julie Ducharme is our featured entrepreneur. She is a TEDx speaker, and the CEO of JD Consulting and several other successful businesses. She is also a bestselling author and professional speaker who specializes in consulting women executives and businesses.

To put it bluntly, she is the epitome of a powerful woman.

Enjoy reading the amazing journey of Dr. Ducharme and learn some of the wealth of wisdom she provides, not only for women, but for everyone.

Also, enjoy motivational stories from the following powerful businesswomen:

Gabrielle Hayes	Kara Mac
Jennifer "JJ" Jank	Ellen Postolowski
Lauren B. Jones	Daniela Schardinger
Sarah Loughry	

PIVOT Magazine

Founder and President
Jason Miller
jason@strategicadvisorboard.com

Editor-in-Chief
Chris O'Byrne
chris@jetlaunch.net

Design
JETLAUNCH.net

Advertising
Chris O'Byrne
chris@jetlaunch.net

Webmaster
Joel Phillips
joel@proshark.com

Editor
Laura West
laura@jetlaunch.net

Cover Design
Debbie O'Byrne

FROM THE DESK OF THE PRESIDENT

In the ever-evolving business world, a new age is emerging: the age of strong, unstoppable women. These entrepreneurial trailblazers are the driving force behind some of the most innovative and successful ventures of our time. Their achievements not only redefine the boundaries of what is possible but also inspire generations to come. As president of a business magazine for women entrepreneurs, I'm in awe of these phenomenal women and their impact in their respective fields.

The entrepreneurship landscape has been changing rapidly, with more women stepping into the spotlight, breaking through the glass ceiling, and seizing opportunities that once seemed out of reach. This wave of women entrepreneurs is challenging conventional wisdom and changing the business world in ways never seen before.

The rise of strong women in entrepreneurship is undoubtedly an encouraging sign of progress. As they conquer their industries, these women are rewriting history, dispelling age-old stereotypes, and proving they have the drive, intelligence, and passion for leading in the competitive business world.

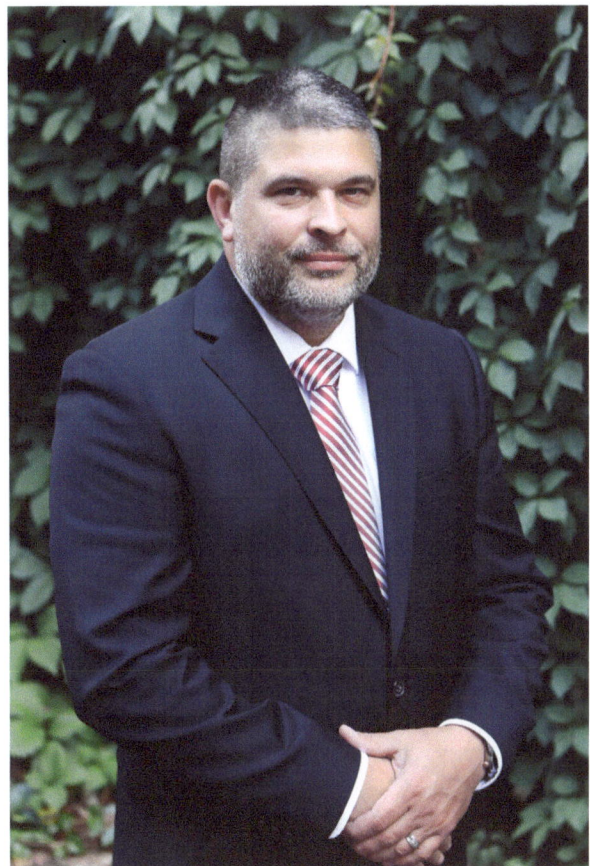

The successes of these women entrepreneurs are more than just a testament to their tenacity and a shining beacon of hope for all who seek to follow in their footsteps. The stories of their resilience, perseverance, and unyielding ambition are invaluable lessons for anyone seeking to build a successful business empire.

From Oprah Winfrey, who turned her love of communications into a billion-dollar media empire, to Indra Nooyi, who led PepsiCo as CEO for twelve years, to Sara Blakely, the founder of Spanx, who became the world's youngest self-made billionaire, there's no shortage of strong women who have broken the glass ceiling.

These inspiring individuals haven't only defied all odds and established themselves as serious forces in the business world. They have repeatedly proven that gender is no barrier to success and that anything is possible with diligence, determination, and a strong vision.

The impact of these strong women goes far beyond their own success stories. They have paved the way for countless women entrepreneurs, inspiring them to pursue their dreams and realize their potential. Their actions have created a ripple effect that touches millions of lives and encourages women worldwide to pursue their goals with confidence and conviction.

But as much as we celebrate these extraordinary achievements, we mustn't forget that there is still a long way to go to achieve gender parity in the business world. Women remain underrepresented in leadership positions, and the gender pay gap remains a significant problem in many industries. So despite the progress made, it's clear that much remains to be done to create a level playing field.

We must continue to support and empower women in entrepreneurship through our admiration and by providing them with the resources and opportunities they need to succeed. Mentoring, education, and access to capital are critical to ensuring that more women can make their mark in the business world.

On the cusp of this new era, I'm in awe of the powerful women who have paved the way for others. Their unyielding determination, strength, and courage remind us of the indomitable spirit within each of us. So let's honor their achievements and be inspired by their stories as we work together to build a more equitable future for all.

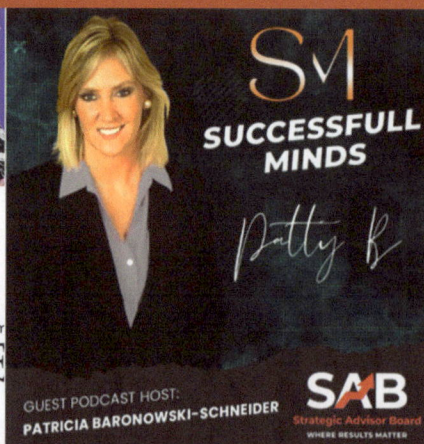

EMPOWERING WOMEN, SERVING VETS, AND CHANGING EDUCATION

DR. JULIE DUCHARME

"Change is never easy but necessary. Expect that, to find success, you will have to face resistance, but resistance creates persistence, and persistence creates success."
–Dr. Julie Ducharme

In my experience, nothing is more powerful than a strong, intelligent woman defying norms, donning a pink tutu, and empowering other women to find their authentic selves. When people ask me how I ended up wearing a pink tutu, I tell them about the day I was reading a book in my office on one hundred things women do wrong in the workplace.

The book advised against having pictures of my family on my desk, talking about my kids, or even having candy around. It essentially said, "Don't be a woman, don't be proud of being a woman, and hide it all." At that moment, I decided to throw the book out. If I couldn't be myself, what was the point? So, I stopped wearing all black with my hair in a bun and glasses and started embracing color and my fun personality. To my delight, people appreciated my leadership style.

Growing up with a father and two grandfathers who owned their own businesses, I have always been surrounded by entrepreneurship. I have been in business since I was eighteen, when I was recruited from my small farm town to play dual sports on a full ride. It was big news for my small town, and I had a lot to prove. After winning a national title, I brought some of my fellow volleyball players and basketball players who had also won back to my hometown to speak to kids about reaching for the stars. I called it Ransom, and we gave motivational talks at schools, empowering children. That's where it all began.

By the time I was twenty-three, I had started my first company. By thirty, I had completed my doctorate, owned three companies, and served as an academic dean for twenty business colleges. I have always been good at looking at an idea and figuring out how to monetize it, and now, after nearly twenty-five years, I have four companies and am often brought in as a consultant on large-scale projects. My latest endeavor is serving as CAO for the Leigh Steinberg Sports Academy.

Despite loving all my businesses, my true passion lies in She Talks. I recall someone telling me about fifteen years ago that I wasn't a big enough celebrity to be on stage and nobody would listen since I hadn't made much money yet. I found this confusing, as colleges paid me to be an expert in a subject and teach people worldwide. I thought, "If you won't give me a platform, I'll make one." That's how She Talks began.

We created a speaking platform and tour about six years ago, where any woman could apply to tell their story without needing to be famous or a multi-millionaire. Now, six years later, we have been in ten different states, trained over eighty women in public speaking, and donated several thousands of dollars to women veterans from our event earnings. As my colleague Dr. Karen Walker says, "We are not your competitor but your biggest supporter." My goal is to empower as many women as I can in my lifetime and help them achieve their highest potential.

I know that women often don't realize their worth, and we have brilliant women hiding in the corner because they don't think they deserve a seat at the table. So, I created a table and welcomed everyone to sit at it. The other driving force behind this was my daughter. I realized I could teach her business, how to make money, and how to be successful—but more importantly, I could teach her how to see her worth and find her "why." Ultimately, you can have all the money in the world and still not be happy, which is why I invest in my passion.

"The only barriers you have are yourself."
–Dr. Julie Ducharme

I empower veterans through my program, Combat Boots to Heels. My good friend and colleague Dr. Karen Walker retired from the military about ten years ago. She confided in me about her struggles with transitioning

to civilian life after twenty years of service, despite having a Ph.D. She mentioned that few programs specifically focused on women's transition. So, we collaborated to create a course that helps women focus on the mentality required for transitioning from military service to civilian life.

In addressing the psychological aspects, we assisted with resumes, interview training, and even interview attire when necessary. In addition, we partnered with several organizations to support veterans in other areas, helping them find the right path to transition instead of pushing them towards another government job, which is a common issue. We have witnessed numerous successes through our program. For example, one woman we helped found her passion for art, while another pursued the education needed to achieve her dream job, ultimately becoming a horse farm owner and yoga instructor. Another woman became a partner in a winery. We take veterans out of the box they've been placed in and present them with options they never knew they had. It's incredibly rewarding to see their "aha" moments.

Our program is housed at Synergy Learning Institute, our technical vocational college, where we offer all our veteran programs. We have also partnered with a university to provide over thirty-five university-accredited courses, many created by transitioning veterans. I am incredibly proud of the college we established, offering quality education at an affordable price while giving students access to true industry experts. I love being an academic disruptor in this way. Most importantly, I strive to create a quality experience in all my businesses. My father taught me that quality is better than quantity—a principle I have carried to all my businesses and passions.

"Some days are so dark I can barely see the light, and some days are so bright I wonder how I could have ever lost sight of the light."
–Dr. Julie Ducharme

Not too long ago, I wrote a book called Authentically You: Empower Your Way to Success. I had spent a good twenty years writing, researching, and publishing on the academic side. This book, however, was a very personal, raw account of my journey, with the hope that I could help others with their journey and help them avoid the tough paths I had to endure. For a long time, I wanted to be perfect Julie, with a perfect body, a perfectly clean house,

picture-perfect children, and a perfect career. Trying to live up to these expectations was exhausting and not true to who I was, but I was lost in the idea of what the world expected me to look and behave like.

I took this pursuit of perfection so extreme that I nearly had a mental breakdown. This experience forced me to look deep inside and figure out who I wanted to be and what I wanted to achieve. When a talented and beautiful friend committed suicide, I realized the importance of being open, honest, and transparent about our struggles so we don't suffer alone. Writing this book was one way I felt I could give back to women by being honest about my own struggles.

The book also offers a thirty-day challenge to help readers find their path and move in

a successful direction. The most important lesson anyone can learn is that if you don't love yourself for who you are, you will struggle with success because you're chasing the wrong kind of success.

One of the most important aspects of my companies and what makes them unique is my life perspective as a "surviving motherhood and working mom." This perspective gives my products and services a unique angle. Experiences from various aspects of life allow me to adapt, be flexible, and problem-solve. As a mother, I'm constantly problem-solving, a skill that transfers to the end customer. When clients come in with a problem, it's usually an easy fix. One of my business's slogans is "your problems, our solutions." My unique situation of having kids and working helps me be the best person to assist all my customers.

I've observed that the happiest and most successful working moms balance life in many areas, not just kids and work. They prioritize their health by integrating time with friends, community events, and hobbies. If all you do is work, you'll burn out quickly. Making time for yourself, your friends, and other aspects of life is essential. Find the balance! Ask yourself if anything will change if you finish a task tonight or tomorrow morning. Usually, the answer is no, but often we women are so consumed with being the best that we don't realize our coworkers are enjoying life while we're still working away at home.

I've been remote working for the last ten years, and finding a break between work and home life is challenging, especially as a workaholic like me. However, I started cutting myself off at a certain time and factoring in playtime with my kids, husband, and myself. These changes made life much more enjoyable. We have to establish boundaries and separate work from home life. For someone like me who works from home, it's tough because I am essentially "on" all the time. I own and run four companies with clients worldwide in different time zones. If I didn't set boundaries, I would never sleep. Establishing these boundaries brought much more balance into my life and household, making me a better boss, owner, wife, and mom.

"Change is never easy but necessary."
–Dr. Julie Ducharme

I have many success stories in my quest to build businesses, empower women, support veterans, and change the education system. One of my favorite stories dates back to when I was coaching a women's college volleyball team. Two girls on the team told me they accidentally got pregnant and probably couldn't stay on the team as they had no support for their babies. I offered my help, and they accepted.

Both girls had babies, continued school full-time, and played for the team. They would drop off their babies with me throughout the week when they went to class, and my husband would often watch them during practice or games. With a little support and someone believing in them, one became an RN, and her son has since graduated high school. The other is a successful elementary school teacher with two more children.

We didn't have She Talks or any support programs back then, but these girls had someone who believed in their success. I think that's what sets me apart from others. When I see potential in my clients, they often just need a guiding hand and someone who believes in them. That's what I provide in all the services and products my companies offer and my passion projects.

There are many ways to work with me or connect. Here are a few: Go to our leadandempowerher.com website and sign up to be a speaker, attendee, or volunteer. Veterans needing help can visit www.synergylearninginstitute.org to check out all our veteran support programs. If you're looking for some university-level courses to better yourself, check out Synergy. If you are a veteran and would like to be featured in one of my national or local veteran transition magazine columns, message me at leadingbymyponytail@gmail.com.

If you would like my business help with websites, podcasting, digital marketing, or course creation, go to jdconsultingsolutions.com. Want to be on one of my podcasts and tell your story? We have my *Authentically You* podcast or my *She CEO Talks*. You can send inquiries or a request to be on the show to leadinbymyponytail@gmail.com.

If you want to co-author a book with me or want a chapter for academia or other publishing, please inquire at leadinbymyponytail@gmail.com.

To help, share our She Talks listed on our YouTube channel called *Leading by my Ponytail*. Word of mouth is the best way for people to learn about us. For social media, I'm on FB as Dr. Julie Ducharme, Instagram as Julie Taylor Ducharme, and LinkedIn as Julie Ducharme. We don't want any of this to be a best-kept secret, so please share.

SHAPING THE NEXT GENERATION OF PRODUCT MANAGERS

GABRIELLE HAYES

I am one of the co-founders of Product x Agile. We're an online learning platform founded specifically for product management teams, product managers, and agilists. We focus on product management and product people as individuals who have either a personal budget or a budget provided by the company to improve their skills in their industry.

Our courses get you up to speed on things like the tools you use daily, communicating with your team, and even how communicating with executives beyond your team or just general knowledge about the industry you're in. But we also have a second layer we focus on with some of our ideal clients, which is growing an entire product team.

So how do we move a team forward? How do we take them to the next level? How do we help them avoid common pitfalls in the industry?

When we look at who our ideal customer is, we either have a person who's in the product business and is hungry for more knowledge and wants to go to the next level and educate themselves, or we have a company that believes in becoming product-centric, solving big customer problems, and will invest in taking their team to the next level.

Whether we're talking about our ideal customer as an individual or our ideal customer as a product team, the issues that challenge them and that they experience are the same. The product management industry is still fairly new, so the career path isn't clearly defined yet. Therefore, the training opportunities and definitions are still vague and hard to grasp.

Sometimes, you find online courses you're interested in, but they may not fit your schedule. They can be pretty rigorous, so you can't arrange your schedule to your own liking, which is difficult. Also, they usually focus on science and theory rather than practice.

What do you do when you finish the course or the cohort-based curriculum? How do you apply what you've learned to your work, and how do you use it to make a difference in your work? Are you actually getting enough value for the money that you're spending?

We make sure that the work and time you put in is meaningful and makes a difference. That way, you're actually able to solve the

challenges and problems you encounter. Your training options making a difference, and you're able to learn and apply what you're learning to your work.

There is no affordable training that is tactical and really gets you ahead. That's why we've partnered with the Kajabi platform to bring you an online training platform that's on-demand and fun. You can take these classes at your own pace on your phone or even in your web browser.

If you want to start a lesson, stop in the middle, and come back—you can do that. We make sure we meet people where they're at and accommodate your schedule. You go at your own pace.

You have unlimited access to the courses once you pay for them. They're always available to you. You also have access to your instructors, and we have "Ask Me Anything" sessions. If you have questions, ask us or ask your community. We're all here to help you and bring it to life for you.

We have an all-in-one platform that gives your company and your product department everything you need to feel strong and grounded in all the work you need to do to have a strong product transition and a strong product organization.

We learned through the product school of hard knocks. Jackie (co-founder) and I both got into product management by accident. That means we learned the hard way, built things the wrong way, and banged our heads every step of the way. We don't want you to do that.

We've spent many, many hours with many, many customers developing the best frameworks and practices for getting products to market to the right people at the right time. We want to change that, and we're passionate about it.

Product-centric businesses are the way of the future. It's the way we stay ahead of the game. It's the way to solve big customer problems and stay in touch with your users. Look at what happened with Southwest Airlines over the holidays. They didn't take care of their products. They didn't take care of the lifecycle. And they failed their users when they needed them most.

That will happen to more and more companies that haven't made the official transition to product orientation, which can only happen with strong, confident, well-trained, tactically minded product managers. We want this world to make that change, and we want to be part of that change.

Jackie and I have been training and doing these personal workshops together for several years. In the summer of 2022, we completed a workshop together in Atlanta. After our last two-day workshop, we went to lunch and took a look at each other. We're both moms, and we both run successful product consulting businesses. We realized we couldn't reach more people if we just limited ourselves to in-person workshops. We love them, and they're a lot of fun, but we know we have expertise that needs to reach more people and can change how products are developed in the world.

The best way to do that is to do what we do best—build a good product. And that's where Product x Agile came from. We've stuck to all the frameworks that we teach. We created a problem value statement; we created a problem canvas; we created a business model; we did user interviews; and we did a business accelerator course to make sure we went through and checked off all the boxes.

We took the same steps we'd recommend to any other company that hires us as a consulting firm or workshop organizer. We've done exactly that to make sure we're reaching the right people at the right time with the right solution.

We're very passionate about Product x Agile. We are changing the product industry, and we help new people grow into that role or feel more confident and efficient in their existing role.

The best thing about what we're doing is that we aren't only changing the way products are brought to market and delivered to users, but we also change lives. We change the way they see their job, their role, and what they do in the world. We're very proud of that.

One of my favorite stories is about a childhood friend of mine. She had just become a mother and was looking for a change and wanted to get into a different industry, but she didn't know how to go about it. She didn't know where to start. She didn't know what that looked like for her. What she knew was that she needed more flexibility in her schedule. She needed something that was a little more creative and fun, and she needed something that supported her family.

She reached out to us and we asked if she wanted to become a Scrum Master and get into product management. We were able to use her as one of our beta customers, walk her through all of our courses, and use her feedback to make some changes to our program. I'm thrilled that she got her first job through our courses. She's able to support her family with a schedule that helps her meet their needs.

Every time I meet with her, I'm so proud to see her grow, to see her skills gain confidence, and to see her keep coming back to us, asking, "What's classes are next. When is the next session? What book are we going to cover next in our book club?" It's so great to see that we've offered her so much that she can't wait to see what we do next. And it's been great to have her feedback help us make the changes we needed to get our program off the ground. It's a mutual-benefit success story I'm very proud of, not only because she's a childhood friend, but also because it helped us launch our business and it helped her launch a new career. It's those career-changing stories that warm my heart that I get to be a part of.

What is the best way to share what we do? Considering that product management is still fairly new, you wouldn't believe how often I get asked this question. Product managers often sit between the business and technical teams to get software and technical products into the industry and to the people who will use them. And that's all of us.

How often use your phone, your computer, your TV, your thermostat—just about anything? Think about cars such as Tesla, where the whole car is a product that product managers are involved in. That's why I tell people that if you want something on your TV fixed faster because it has a bug, and you don't like the way it works, file a customer complaint. You want someone on the other end of the line to listen to that customer complaint, talk to the developers, and make sure the problem gets fixed faster so you can release it faster. That's what a product manager does. We take information, research it, translate it so that the technical team can implement it, and then decide when we can release it to our users.

So that's what I mean when I say that we train people in how to get the information out faster and more efficiently and get it to users when they want it and need it. That's why it's so important we have more product managers who are confident in their role. We want them to do the discovery; we want them to do the research; we want them to talk to the users; and we want them to develop the products faster and get them to market sooner.

That's why training for product managers is so important. We need more of them in the industry. If you're thinking about it, please get in touch. We'd love to tell you what this role and career path could look like because it's desperately needed. We're going to need more people in this industry in the future; I can promise you that.

But it's also fun. We build things from the ground up. Often, ideas turn into real products that people use. It's a great mix of being a project manager and being creative at the same time. It's being creative and drawing things on the back of a napkin and then seeing them come to life on a computer screen or a phone screen.

And that's exactly what a product manager's job is. I have had the opportunity to be on the front lines, training them and bringing them up to speed because our industry is still changing, which is a lot of fun.

If you see any software or technology asking for your feedback or if you get an email asking you to fill out a survey, I urge you to take a few minutes and do that. Those of us who work in product management use user resource searches and user feedback to decide what we develop next for the product. I know that sometimes it feels exhausting, and sometimes it's just another item on your to-do list.

But I promise you, if it's a product you like—your TV, your phone, your computer, your car—please consider these surveys. They help us make informed decisions and remove assumptions from our products. As a product manager, you, the user, are on the front lines of everything we do. That's why your input is so important to us. Please support us as a community to make sure we're developing the right thing at the right time for the right person—you.

If you're interested in one of our courses, you can find them at productxagile.com. You have lifetime access to them, so once you buy them, they're saved in your account, and you can look them up as often as you need.

If you have a product team or would like to talk about courses, personal workshops, or coaching, contact us at hello@productxagile.com and send us a few notes about your situation and what you want so we can work together to figure out what your scenario might look like.

We're also very active on Instagram, where we're always posting up-to-date product content, tips and tricks, and additional skills and information. If you're not ready to take a class yet, but want to see what product management is about, follow us on Instagram at @productxagile and join in. I look forward to connecting with you!

THE NEUROSCIENCE OF PRODUCTIVITY

JENNIFER "JJ" JANK

My career path has been quite nonlinear. Although I often mention my twenty-year tenure in finance, I engaged in many activities during that time. Over the last decade, I worked as a financial planner in corporate America, consistently completing my tasks more quickly than my peers.

I could put my head down and work in a way that others weren't, which is why I could get everything done quickly. What I didn't realize until I started researching brain science was that I was always naturally working with my brain. This is countercultural because the prevailing culture is very anti-brain and not helpful at all.

You want to be working with your brain, and I was contrarian enough that I did everything the way I wanted to do it because I wanted to get my tasks completed. Corporate America annoyed me because they wanted me to sit at my desk for eight hours. If I finished my work in five hours, why couldn't I go home and enjoy my life instead of sitting at my desk for three more hours? A lot of aspects of corporate America didn't work for me, and that was definitely one of them.

After leaving corporate America, I pursued writing—a passion I'd maintained throughout my career—and began delving into neuroscience. As a self-proclaimed nerd, I find the brain's workings utterly fascinating. One of the best aspects of my current focus is that our understanding of the brain will continue to evolve during my lifetime, ensuring that I'll constantly be learning and discovering new things.

Eventually, I grasped why my productivity surpassed that of my peers. It seemed natural, albeit nonlinear, to use my newfound knowledge to help others boost their productivity. One of the most rewarding aspects of my work is when people tell me they can enjoy spending time with their families without feeling guilty about being away from their jobs. We need to make time for play.

Unfortunately, in today's culture, adults often feel they're not allowed to have fun. However, when people realize that leisure activities can enhance their productivity, they're more likely to engage in them. Therefore, I advocate for "unproductive productivity"—activities that replenish one's productivity reserves, such as playing games, having fun, going for walks, exercising, eating well, and getting enough sleep.

These practices might not sound like productivity boosters, but they're vital for long-term success. Rather than focusing on time-saving tricks, such as mastering keyboard shortcuts, I emphasize the importance of activities that might not seem work-related. Our work-centric culture often makes people feel guilty for taking time off, but leisure activities can improve performance the following day.

This counterintuitive and countercultural approach resonates with me. I relish the opportunity to help others permit themselves to enjoy life, ultimately benefiting their overall productivity.

My ideal customers are business owners who have reached a plateau in profit or revenue. They may feel they have most of the right people and systems in place, but something is blocking their progress. Often, they believe they're paying their employees enough, but they're not getting the desired level of productivity from everyone.

These business owners may have employees who procrastinate or lack a clear understanding of their roles. As a result, there could be systems that need revising, or their methods for delegating work aren't as efficient as they could be. I specialize in working with women business owners and collaborate with men. I'm seeking clients eager to identify and address productivity gaps in their businesses.

However, my ideal clients are not those who push their employees to work excessive hours or hire indiscriminately, hoping that more staff will automatically lead to better results. Instead, my primary focus is on business owners struggling with a plateau and committed to finding solutions to improve their productivity.

Typically, the business owners I work with are in professional services, such as lawyers, accountants, and financial planners. As a former financial planner, I'm very familiar with the finance aspect of these industries. Therefore, I focus on helping those whose businesses require them and their staff to engage in cognitively demanding work, such as working with spreadsheets, developing strategies, or creating financial plans and tax returns.

I also work with marketing agency owners, supporting tasks that demand significant mental effort. My services are not aimed at retail or hospitality business owners, as the nature of their work is different from the cognitively challenging tasks I help clients with. My goal is to improve productivity for my clients, allowing them and their employees to achieve a healthy work-life balance without having to work longer hours.

I emphasize the importance of not creating arbitrary tasks just to have something to check off a to-do list. Instead, I encourage clients to focus on a small number of actionable items that, when completed, will move them forward in their careers or help their businesses grow. By concentrating on these significant tasks, clients can make real progress toward achieving their goals.

I primarily work with clients who have reached a plateau in their businesses. They've already addressed the easy fixes, such as upgrading from calculators to spreadsheets or utilizing purchased software. Despite making these small adjustments, they still struggle to break through the ceiling, whether in profit or revenue. These clients understand that productivity isn't about being busy but working towards goals that will advance their businesses. However, they're getting stuck and can't pinpoint the productivity gaps.

To help these clients, I offer several solutions, starting with assessments. My approach is similar to management consulting, where I examine their various processes to identify gaps in productivity. My clients typically have established and successful businesses generating six to seven figures in revenue but aim for even higher earnings. As a result, they don't believe they need to hire more people or force their staff into working fourteen-hour days. Instead, they want to uncover the productivity gaps that will enable them to reach their next goals and break through the plateau.

Often, these business owners suspect that some employees could be more productive but haven't reached their full potential for various reasons. They may have a clue of what's holding these individuals back or may be completely in the dark. Sometimes, it's difficult for business owners to step back and work *on* their businesses rather than only *in* them. Additionally, many clients were once accountants, financial planners, or marketers who now run their own firms, lacking prior experience in streamlining back-office operations or understanding available systems.

My role is to help these business owners identify and address productivity gaps in their employees or systems. In most cases, the issue is a combination of both. By offering my expertise, I enable clients to solve these problems and propel their businesses forward.

I offer two main services: a consulting solution and a half-day workshop. The half-day workshop is designed for smaller companies to get started on productivity. While my core clients have already tackled the basic steps, those attending the workshop may not have, or their staff might still be working on them. In addition, the workshop introduces participants to the idea that productivity resides mainly in the brain, debunking popular myths and misconceptions.

Understanding productivity is crucial; it's not just about being busy or using countless productivity apps. Relying on too many apps can worsen the situation. The workshop also covers topics like the inability to multitask during cognitively demanding work, structuring one's day to maximize "thinky" work time, and prioritizing tasks. Helping people learn how to prioritize is a significant aspect of the workshop.

I offer consulting services for larger clients, typically those with six and seven-figure revenues. This involves examining processes, process mapping, and identifying productivity gaps. We often deal with systems and people, addressing issues such as ineffective prioritization, improper work schedules, and suboptimal systems. The focus is on creating more efficient and effective processes for the clients.

Later in the year, I plan to launch a program that emphasizes accountability, though I hesitate to call it a mastermind. Clients receive steps to implement necessary changes with traditional management consulting, but often nothing happens months down the line. This new program will provide a structured approach to discussing productivity issues and ensuring accountability for taking action to move businesses forward.

What I offer is not technically management consulting; it's productivity consulting. However, I do utilize the management consulting framework as a foundation. One benefit of this approach is examining operations and processes as a whole through the lens of productivity. I focus on the people and systems involved, identifying areas for improvement and bottlenecks.

In one consulting job I did, the owner and founder turned out to be the biggest obstacle to productivity in their company. Having a productivity expert with an objective viewpoint can be invaluable. I won't recommend an excessive number of applications or focus on trivial aspects. Instead, I examine the overall systems and strategize on how to enhance them.

The principles of productivity are fairly simple, but our society is often designed to be counterproductive and distracting. That's why the consulting framework, which emphasizes change management, works well in this context. But first, it's crucial to recognize that productivity resides in the brain, and that modern culture often distracts us from our tasks.

To break through the plateau, companies must learn how to engineer their environment to reduce distractions and structure their day for maximum productivity. Focusing on those two or three essential tasks that propel the business forward is key to achieving greater success.

The half-day workshop I offer is highly valuable due to its interactive nature. For instance, I include a fun quiz where participants discover their sleep chronotypes, allowing managers to gain insights into their team's optimal work hours. For example, if a team consists primarily of "bears," who perform best between 9:00 a.m. and 1:00 p.m., managers should avoid sending urgent emails or scheduling meetings during those hours. The same applies to other chronotypes like lions, wolves, and dolphins. Understanding these differences can help departments coordinate meetings and communication better to minimize distractions and boost productivity.

I once visited a client's office and found an employee using a calculator in front of a computer. It was a clear example of how proper training on software tools can lead to significant improvements in efficiency. Spreadsheets have been around for decades and utilizing them can eliminate the need for manual calculations. Unfortunately, a lack of training on available software often results in wasted time and resources.

Having worked for software firms while in finance, I am familiar with various software solutions and understand the types of reports businesses require. Even if I haven't encountered specific software, I can usually deduce whether it contains the information clients need.

The best way for someone to start working with me is to book a free half-hour consultation. We discuss where you feel stuck and what's happening during this time. While thirty minutes isn't a long time, it usually provides enough information for me to determine if we will be a good fit. Additionally, I maintain collaborative relationships with various professionals, such as HR generalists, staffing companies, and software-operations experts. If a client requires a deeper dive than my productivity

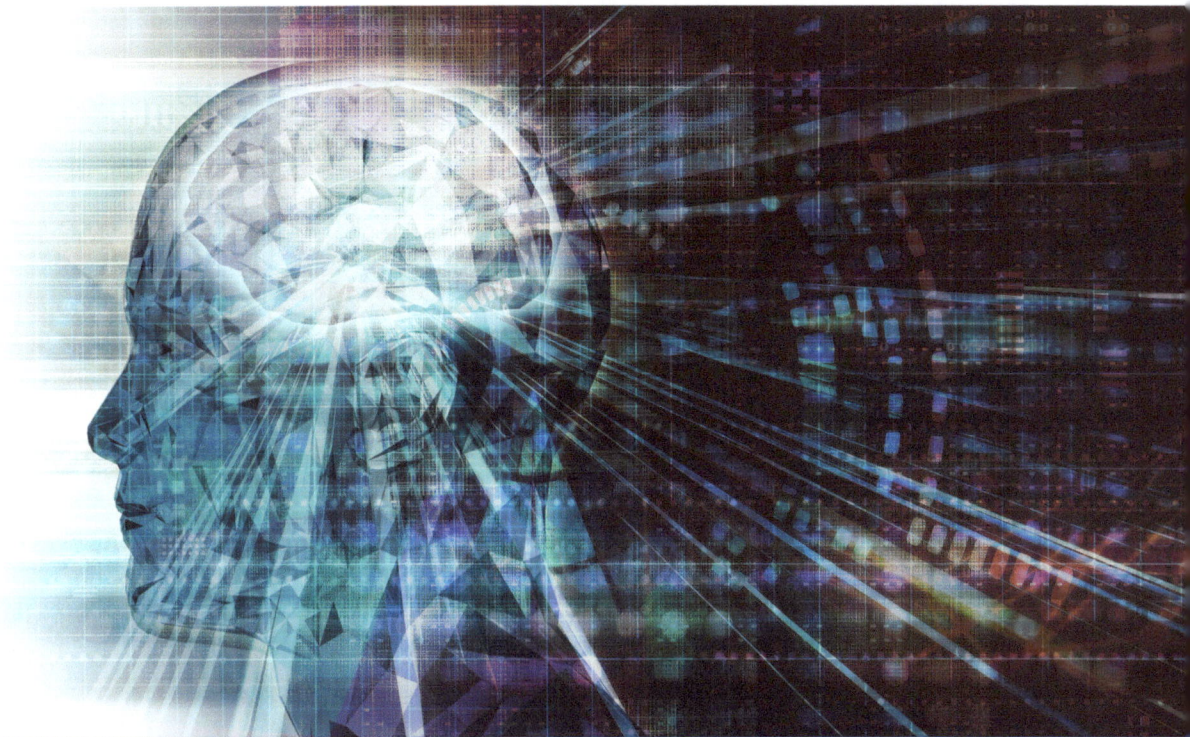

consultation offers, I can refer them to one of these specialists.

Moreover, I regularly share content on LinkedIn under Jennifer "JJ" Jank and on my website, jenniferjank.com. Both platforms feature weekly blog updates and details about my workshops and consultations. I encourage people to explore my written content because solopreneurs or individuals who may not be ideal clients for my workshop or consultation might find valuable insights in my blog posts and LinkedIn articles. For example, while my ideal business owner clients won't find complete solutions in my blog, they can still benefit from learning about sleep chronotypes or managing distractions.

For those who need more assistance than my content provides, I'm happy to conduct a half-hour consultation to explore how I can serve.

I truly appreciate referrals and am quite active on LinkedIn. I encourage people to repost my content and share it with their own audience. For those who have worked with me, discussing their experiences with others in similar situations can be helpful. However, I understand that it might be challenging for some to know exactly who to talk to about my services, so sharing my LinkedIn posts is a convenient alternative.

Additionally, I send out two newsletters each month. The mid-month edition typically focuses on a specific productivity topic, providing actionable takeaways—for example, this month's topic deals with distractions. At the end of the month, I offer a roundup summarizing the month's events, upcoming items, and various articles or resources I've come across that may interest my audience. Forwarding these newsletters can be another excellent way for people to share information about my work.

One of the key concepts I often emphasize is that if something is good for the brain, it's good for productivity. This is crucial to understand because productivity begins in the brain. I like to think of the brain as containing a little productivity tank that gets depleted as we engage in cognitively demanding tasks. So, for example, attempting to multitask—although not a real possibility—only exhausts the brain and drains the productivity tank.

To refill this tank, working fourteen-hour days is not the solution. Instead, activities such as exercise, proper nutrition, getting enough sleep, engaging in playtime, and spending time with friends and family can all contribute to a more productive mindset. As an introvert, I often joke about our need for social connection. While introverts may require less social interaction than extroverts, it's still essential for all of us to connect with others to thrive as a species.

In essence, if it's good for the brain, it's good for productivity. This concept is similar to understanding the importance of eating nutritious food. While people may not always make healthy choices, everyone generally knows the difference between nutritious and unhealthy options, like a fast-food burger with extra-large fries.

One aspect that often resonates with people is when I discuss distractions and assure them that it's not their fault they're easily distracted. Being distracted doesn't necessarily mean you have ADHD or are losing cognitive function due to age. We are constantly bombarded with an overwhelming amount of information, far more than our parents ever had to deal with, and it's only getting worse.

Social media platforms, while seemingly social, are designed to exploit our brain's addictive tendencies to keep us engaged and exposed to advertisements. These ads are specifically created to be distracting, pulling our focus away from our tasks. People need to understand that being frequently distracted is not a personal failure. Instead, overcoming distractions requires deliberate effort and intentionality.

As someone who falls on the extremely productive end of the spectrum, I employ various techniques that may not be considered the norm in corporate America. For example, I don't answer emails immediately, avoid checking emails before starting my day, and don't allow interruptions when I need to focus. While not everyone in a company can adopt these practices, one can still take measures to enhance productivity. However, it's essential to recognize that you might not reach maximum productivity, and that's all right. Maintaining a certain level of connectedness is a personal choice and a trade-off. Ultimately, the decision is yours to make.

About the Author

Jennifer "JJ" Jank helps business owners and their teams pump up profits without putting in more hours at work. Her goal is to help entrepreneurs, especially women, engineer their businesses to be more productive so everyone in the company achieves optimal work-life balance.

GROW YOUR BUSINESS WITH STAFFING

LAUREN B. JONES

Our ideal customers are staffing and recruiting agencies of all sizes, from start-ups to enterprise-level organizations, with a strong need for technology, process, and training to support their growth. These agencies typically struggle in three key areas.

The Build Phase is the first of these areas, as agencies face the challenge of making well-informed decisions amidst a $17.5 billion industry of work, HR, and staffing tech.

Our business is technology, and our team has decades of experience helping companies understand their actual needs rather than being swayed by savvy software sales experts. As a result, we ensure agencies acquire the technology they need, exactly when and how they need it.

The second area of struggle is the Process Phase. When firms transition from one technology to another, they often try to make the new tech work like the old tech, preventing them from utilizing the full potential of their new tools. This approach also inhibits growth through over-customization. We help agencies understand the capabilities of new technology and redefine their processes to streamline operations and foster growth in the right way.

Finally, the Adoption Phase presents a significant challenge to the industry. While a considerable amount of technology is purchased, adoption rates remain low. Our solution is to create bespoke training content designed with microlearning principles in mind, ensuring that new technology becomes an integral part of the agency's daily operations.

In today's world, staffing is about relationships powered and empowered by technology. Recruiting businesses that engage with LEAP Consulting Solutions share a common need: optimizing their use of technology to create better experiences and achieve successful business outcomes. They seek help in making this a reality, and that's where LEAP Consulting Solutions steps in, with a mission to make recruiting companies more efficient, more successful, and more human.

Founder and CEO Lauren Jones has a passion for technology that drives her curiosity to help firms understand and harness the power of workforce tech in meaningful ways. A significant aspect of this success lies in managing change for people and systems and redesigning business operations for maximum efficiency and effectiveness. Lauren's expertise extends beyond her work at LEAP.

Lauren is a frequent speaker, podcast co-host, and author, sharing her knowledge on recruitment technology, business operations, change management, and women's issues. Her insights are valued within the industry, and she is a sought-after resource. For more information about LEAP Consulting Solutions and how it can benefit your staffing agency, visit leapconsultingsolutions.com.

What sets our team apart from others is our wealth of experience and expertise. With over twenty-five years of managing profitable and successful enterprise staffing firms, our team members deeply understand the industry. Furthermore, they have accumulated over thirty-five years of experience in staffing tech implementation and development. In addition, they have over twenty-five years of training and successful adoption experience under their belts.

Our team's passion, drive, and unwavering devotion to the success of our agency distinguish us from the rest. We are committed to providing the best solutions for our clients' needs.

Lauren Jones is a staffing industry powerhouse, workforce technology expert, change management mastermind, fierce leader, and professional storyteller. As the founder and CEO of LEAP Consulting Solutions, she has made it her mission to help recruiting companies become more efficient, successful, and human. She achieves this by assisting firms in defining and understanding their technology needs, embracing change, and optimizing their technology investments.

Lauren is a respected voice on staffing, technology, entrepreneurship, and women's leadership. She recently co-authored her first book, "Together We Rise," a collection of personal stories about women's empowerment, alongside several industry peers. Her reputation has earned her guest appearances on many recruiting industry podcasts, such as Settle Smarter, You Own the Experience Podcast (which she now co-hosts), TheEdge, Ivy Podcast, Staffing Hub, HR Lift Off, and more. As a sought-after speaker, Lauren has presented at top recruitment industry events like Staffing World, the TechServe Executive Summit, CSP, Alternative Staffing Alliance, Staffing Industry Analysts Executive Forum, The World Staffing Summit, and Bullhorn Engage.

Some of her career highlights include receiving the ASA Care Award for connecting veterans with work opportunities, being named a LinkedIn Inspiring Woman in 2022, and being featured on the 2021 lists of the Top 15 Staffing Professionals and Top 200 Thought Influencers to Watch. Lauren's endless curiosity and deep commitment to helping others are fueled by her passion for community activism, involvement in organizations like the National Charity League, Women's Empowerment, and Saint John's Program, and her love for Peloton rides. A proud mother of two successful daughters, Emily and Allison, Lauren lives on a farm in Elk Grove, California, with her husband, Peter.

With a client base of over twenty customers, LEAP Consulting Solutions has helped hundreds of firms successfully navigate the three phases of digital transformation through their Build, Change, Adopt approach.

Remember, you're never too old to chase your dreams.

Contact me on LinkedIn, where I'm known as the "GOAT Leader" and hard to miss. You can also visit our website at: leapconsultingsolutions.com or email lauren@leapconsultingsolutions.com. Finally, if you're feeling adventurous, try reaching me by carrier pigeon!

Search for the hashtag #techstackqueen to find all the content you need to share. And always remember our three guiding principles: Build, Change, Adopt. We assist you in building the systems necessary for success, guide you through change the right way, and help you achieve the ROI on your valuable investment in technology.

About the Author

Lauren Jones is a powerful voice in the staffing industry, sharing her expertise in recruitment technology, business operations, change management, and women's issues as a frequent speaker, podcast co-host, author, and entrepreneur.

CHASING THE DREAM: AN INTERVIEW WITH EM DASH CEO

SARAH LOUGHRY

Sarah Loughry makes things happen. She's a writer, editor, SEO expert, founder, and CEO of Em Dash Blogging, and every now and again she even has a moment to spend with her darling 4-year-old daughter Lennon before jetting off to speak at a retreat somewhere out in the world.

And slyly tucked in between it all? An occasional glass of wine. (White. Or Red. Either.)

She's very hard to catch because she gives everything to her clients, but fortunately, she was able to squeeze us in to talk about all things Em Dash, entrepreneurial, and up-and-coming in the world of optimized SEO and high-quality content production.

Where does the road to Em Dash begin for you?

Sarah: I never do anything halfway. It probably gets me into trouble! When I started out in corporate marketing, I was young and already dreaming of C-suite. But when I finally got there, I discovered—to my horror—that the rest of my life was going to be sitting in boardrooms, dozing off in meetings with people that didn't value my input.

So what do you do? Start dreaming again. I left, and never looked back.

What led you to content and SEO?

Sarah: I always wanted to be a writer, but I never thought I had what it took. Once I left corporate all bets were off, so I took a remote job with an e-commerce startup. With startups the budgets are low or non-existent, so I had to learn how to generate organic traffic, and that naturally introduced me to SEO and blogging. All of a sudden, there I was: discovering writing.

I fell in love immediately and started freelancing to get more experience. It was fast-paced, exciting, new every day—I would quickly pivot from an art topic to the effects of the keto diet on your body. I ended up at a boutique digital marketing agency helping to build their blog service line and that grew into a Senior Manager role where I worked across all clients. It was a dream and I heavily attribute that to the incredible team (shout out to Axle Eight).

But you left?

Sarah: Well, here's the flip side to achieving your dreams: they also evolve. I cherished

the people and I lived and died for the work, but I knew deep down that it wouldn't last forever. That sounds cynical but it's true. And I know I wanted my own company. So I started Em Dash Blogging as a side hustle.

From the editing job, I knew nobody was really targeting content for small or medium-sized businesses. The problem was the price point. At that time, the content and SEO industry was geared for big companies, and it was cost prohibitive for the small fish to get in the game. By consolidating everything I'd learned, I was able to create a business model that offered a holistic solution aimed at their market space.

It looks like it worked.

Sarah: Well, it was a little more complicated than that. In the freelance world, there's a lot of mediocre writing out there. A LOT.

Marrying SEO to content in a way that resonates is a bit alchemical. Sure, you can pay someone $20 to shove a keyword into a blog 50 times and it might help you rank, but it won't be a quality piece.

I realized early on that the biggest value I could offer my clients was better writing.

It's been the bedrock philosophy of Em Dash since day 1, and it's the first advice I give to anyone starting a new business: quality first.

The first line on your site is "The writing agency sent to save your blog's soul". I love that.

Sarah: Exactly. Affordable price, high-quality product. That's what we're all about.

What services do you offer?

Sarah: Today, we're an end-to-end solution for content. We have some clients for whom we focus on full-on content strategy. Social media posts, blog content, email nurtures–all of it, and we make sure everything is harmonized to reach their overall KPIs.

Our bread and butter is writing articles to help our clients rank on Google, and we have specific packages for that. Initially, we do a lot of interviewing to get aligned with exactly what the client wants. After that, we do keyword research to find the best targets for the strategy. We map out a content calendar with recommended blog topics, web content, or both depending on the client, and if it looks good, we start writing. Then we wait for the data to start pouring in, analyze, and adjust.

Do you do website work as well?

Sarah: Absolutely. Like I said, we're an end-to-end solution, and website audits are a crucial part of generating organic traffic. We do monthly assessments and give all our clients a 30 minute to one-hour monthly consultation to go over the numbers and evaluate strategy moving forward.

Additionally, we started expanding our copywriting service line to help a business's overall branding and on page SEO. Today, it's a major part of what we do. We help with landing pages, social media, captions, white papers, case studies, and pretty much anything content-wise you can imagine.

Who's your ideal client?

Sarah: Our ideal clients are people who have been in business for about two to five years. That's about how long it takes to get established enough to have both the budget (even small) and the vision for what you want your content to be. By that point, they'll have the founder and CEO, possibly a marketing director, and they're closing in on six to seven figures. They're ready for a company like Em Dash to step in for content.

What are your clients looking for?

Sarah: The main pain points for the customers we work with are time and SEO knowledge. Creating content is really hard and takes a long time, and it's unrealistic to think a founder is going to have time to write, research, optimize, and post.

Also, as Google continues to evolve its algorithm, quality is becoming more and more important. Remember, this isn't just writing, which is hard enough. This is about writing well AND optimizing for search. You have to do both, not one of the other.

That must require educating clients, too.

Sarah: Our three main values are quality, affordability, and transparency. There is a lot of confusion around SEO, and a lot of companies don't do a great job of explaining exactly why something works and why you should do it. We take the time to fill our clients in because they deserve to understand the strategy we're bringing to them.

What's your biggest success story to date?

Sarah: A success story for me is getting someone on page one of Google for something that we wrote or a keyword we're targeting, and ideally in the top five results. We've had several clients land there which is really exciting, but there's one in particular we're really proud of.

We started working with them last May, And they weren't getting any organic traffic at all. Normally, depending on the space and the keywords you're targeting, it takes at least ten months to start ranking. Not on page one—just to rank.

Also, they were a social media ad agency, and the marketing space is saturated. They're competing with giants like Neil Patel and HubSpot. So, we took a very specific content approach with them, and we ended up increasing the organic traffic to their site by 280% in just the last eight or nine months.

We're ranking for several blogs and hundreds of keywords now by simply writing three targeted blog posts a month. It's been extremely successful. I'm very proud of it, and just thrilled to see it's continuing to grow.

Any new dreams on the horizon?

Sarah: Always, but all of them involve Em Dash! Working with clients I truly believe in fills my cup. It makes our team happy to work with people doing great things in the world.

I'm able to partner with incredible brands and incredible entrepreneurs, and I'm constantly surrounded by people who have the same vivid passion for their work as I do.

That resonates with us at Em Dash. We're passionate people. We believe in our clients' products and we're going to push it as far as we can for them, because when you dream big, the sky's the limit.

VERSATILITY AND SUSTAINABILITY IN WOMEN'S SHOES

KARA MAC

Catering to the busy woman aged thirty to fifty-five, I provide shoes that accommodate her love for fashion, versatility, and quality while staying in harmony with sustainability. She values comfort and practicality and is delighted to find multiple looks in just one pair of shoes. This woman seeks the ultimate shoe that can do it all.

Typically, a woman has nineteen pairs of shoes in her collection, but many remain unworn. Our customers struggled to find comfortable footwear that could seamlessly transform between styles and adapt to their outfits. Now, they can minimize their environmental impact while enhancing their wardrobe and contributing to a greener planet. Our range of high-quality, comfortable shoes, sandals, and boots offers our

For twenty-five years, I served as a design director in the apparel industry, facing a problem I knew wasn't unique to me. It became clear I needed to apply my skills and experience to solve this issue. During my daily commute to New York City, I had separate shoes for commuting, a dozen pairs under my desk, and another pair in my shoulder bag for evening events. I searched for versatile shoes that could transition between different looks but found none.

I couldn't believe I was the only woman facing this challenge, so I scoured the internet for a shoe designer who had addressed this problem. When I couldn't find any solutions, I created one myself. To validate my idea, I had the rare opportunity to meet with serial entrepreneur and investor Daymond John, well-known from the TV series Shark Tank. His faith in my idea encouraged me to leave my corporate career and fully dedicate myself to building the company.

Working from home, I initially started with one heel height and shape on three shoe styles. Kara Mac Shoes was launched in 2015 at a large women's conference. Over the years, I added more heel shapes and heights to the lineup as I gathered proof of concept, sales, and repeat customers. By 2017, I earned a utility patent from the

USPTO, followed by a stronger one a year later. Today, Kara Mac Shoes offers four heel shapes and ten classic shoe styles in our collection.

This year is exciting for the company as we produce every shoe style using eco-friendly materials. Our first sustainable offerings are revamped versions of our most popular boots, the Broadway and the Betty Boot 2.0. These durable boots last a long time, and once discarded, biodegrade 90% faster than traditional leather shoes. This collection is being crowdfunded on I Fund Women (ifundwomen.com/projects/kara-mac-shoes-eco-friendly-womens-boots), and customers can pre-order now to receive a $100 discount and be among the first to receive them in early October 2023.

Supporting others is rewarding, but uplifting women holds a special place in my heart. Therefore, I have chosen Dress for Success as my preferred charity for four years. This organization provides work attire, shoes, and accessories to women re-entering the workforce after facing hardships, such as domestic abuse, caretaking responsibilities, or other life-altering circumstances. With every pair of shoes purchased from us, we donate a pair to Dress for Success, a gesture that brings me immense joy.

As the sole fashion designer in my community, I take pride in mentoring high school students through a program called WISE. I guide these ambitious seniors who dream of studying fashion or art in college as they complete internships with us.

Embarking on the entrepreneurial journey isn't for everyone; it requires courage and resilience. Yet, if you possess a dream, a vision, and find passion in your daily work, I wholeheartedly encourage you to pursue it.

About the Author

Kara envisioned a way to lessen footwear's environmental impact by repurposing existing components, extending their lifespan, reducing landfill waste, and lightening the load in her work bag. In 2015, Kara Mac Shoes debuted, featuring an innovative Click-and-Snap heel cover system, allowing for the effortless transformation of a single pair of boots by switching out fashionable heel covers. Catering to women who value versatility, sustainability, and a single shoe that does it all, the patented invention presents the world's first instantly customizable shoe line, from heel to toe. With various stylish, playful, and personalized options dubbed "Candy," users can effortlessly re-style their shoes to suit their unique preferences. Learn more at KaraMac.com.

GUT DRIVEN: UNCOVERING THE BODY'S HIDDEN CONNECTIONS

ELLEN POSTOLOWSKI

My story begins about thirty years ago when I started working as a nutrition-based chef. I have cooked meals for private clients for most of my life, helping them develop better eating habits. Then, about seven years ago, I felt the need to reinvent Chef Ellen and evolve.

As I got older, I grew tired of constantly being in the kitchen and on my feet. So, I decided to go back to school for integrative nutrition. Since I was already coaching clients to some extent, I wanted to obtain the proper certifications to guide them with food-related choices more effectively. Thus, I developed my reset program.

While in school, I learned about a more integrative approach that considers the whole body. For example, instead of solely focusing on the nourishing aspects of food on one's plate, I delved deeper into gut and hormonal health. This holistic perspective allowed me to expand my expertise and better serve my clients.

My "aha" moment occurred when I became my first client. While in school, I experienced several health issues that I had initially normalized, but they eventually began to take a toll on my well-being. I was diagnosed with early-onset osteoporosis, and my doctors wanted to put me on medications immediately. Moreover, my body was not properly absorbing nutrients, so I needed to address these underlying problems.

I sought to understand why this was happening to me at such a young age, but I wasn't finding the answers I needed. It took finding the right professionals and combining the marvels of modern medicine with a more holistic approach to determine why certain things were happening within my body.

Becoming my first client and discovering all these fascinating aspects of how the body functions—such as the digestive tract breaking down foods, how it feeds hormones, and how it controls cognitive functions in the brain—motivated me to share this knowledge with my clients. Eventually, I decided to share it with the world, leading to the creation of my book, *Gut Driven*.

My product, primarily the information and program detailed in my book, could be the best solution for my clients because I work with them one-on-one, emphasizing that we are all individuals with unique physiologies, makeups, needs, and upbringings. The notion that what works for someone else may not necessarily be in your best interest is a significant component of the solutions I provide for my customers.

I offer a comprehensive program with tips, tricks, menus, and recipes. Some clients may struggle with symptoms that could be food-related, and I aim to break that down to determine what might be causing specific issues, such as bloating or discomfort after eating.

Working with clients, I strive to pinpoint potential sensitivities or intolerances related to food or digestion. As a result, I can help clients improve their overall well-being by addressing these issues and develop a healthier relationship with food.

My program breaks down the science behind how the human body perceives stress. Whether you're feeding that stress with something like a sugar addiction or lack of self-care, these factors accumulate. I explore various aspects of what could be driving inflammation in the body, along with ways to handle stress and inflammation and work on finding solutions to health issues.

It's possible to reduce stress, but eliminating it is difficult. Stress contributes to inflammation, so learning to manage it effectively can help reduce inflammation, leading to better overall health.

We live in a time when numerous chronic and autoimmune illnesses are prevalent. Unfortunately, many people may not fully grasp the importance of ridding their bodies of inflammation. While you may not feel the effects now, inflammation can eventually catch up with you and impact your health in the long run.

My clients typically include individuals unhappy with their current situation, whether it involves trying to eat well or finding ways to improve their diet. These clients often seek guidance and someone to help them stay accountable in reaching their goals. Much of my work involves checking in with clients, holding weekly meetings, and solving problems.

My book, *Gut Driven: Jump-Start Digestive Health to Nourish Body, Mind, and Spirit,* focuses on the intricate digestive system and the importance of paying attention to symptoms such as poor sleep, anxiety, bloating, or rashes. These issues could be food-related, or something else is happening in the body that needs to be addressed.

When working with clients, I guide them in the right direction or refer them to a professional who offers a more holistic approach. By doing so, we usually make progress with their pain or struggles, ultimately finding solutions rather than merely normalizing the discomfort that so many people tend to live with.

I typically begin by going through a comprehensive health history with my clients to pinpoint specific goals and identify any red flags I might want to address. Then, I use a program that eliminates potentially inflammatory foods for three weeks. This approach can benefit individuals struggling with sleepless nights, sugar cravings, constant bloating, or other concerns. It helps calm the body and delve deeper into identifying underlying causes. We may even uncover potential sensitivities or intolerances.

This three-week program has proven to be quite effective, and by the end, clients often establish a foundation for better food choices. However, I also examine other aspects of their lives, such as ongoing stressors like a demanding relative or a tendency to prioritize others' needs over their own. I guide my clients toward incorporating more self-care practices that bring them joy and encourage them to focus on taking care of themselves first. This approach is reminiscent of the airplane safety instructions that advise passengers to secure their own oxygen masks before assisting others.

I assist clients with self-care practices, food choices, and other concerns they may be experiencing. The issues are often food-related, and I believe many problems originate in our gut, which is connected to our brain and hormonal activity. Hormonal activity plays a significant role in the body's happiness, dopamine, and serotonin levels. About 90% of serotonin is produced in the gut.

By addressing gut issues and making better choices—such as avoiding processed foods, additives, and preservatives—we can spark a snowball effect of positive changes across the board. This includes becoming conscientious label readers and reducing our reliance on convenience foods.

My ideal customer would be someone looking to make positive, sustainable changes concerning their health. I aim to educate and guide my clients to feel their best by embracing self-care practices. As a nutrition-based chef and health coach, I consider the food on the plate and the "food" that nourishes you off the plate.

This concept, known as primary food, can include relationships, stress, spirituality, current job situation, or any aspect of your life that you may not be entirely satisfied with and wish to change. I assist and guide my clients in identifying areas that may not serve them well and help them make positive, lasting changes.

I've had numerous success stories with clients, and one that stands out involves a client who suffered from chronic migraines. These migraines were so debilitating that she would have to stay in a dark room for one or two days. We began working together, and by eliminating inflammatory foods for three weeks, she was able to identify several factors that helped her reduce the frequency of her migraines significantly. While she still experiences them occasionally, her progress has been remarkable. She became an avid label reader and shifted away from relying on convenience foods and bars, which has greatly helped with her migraines.

I often work with people who have endured significant discomfort in their bodies. We tend to normalize these issues and live with the discomfort, but it doesn't have to be that way. A significant aspect of my practice involves helping clients understand the importance of finding what works best. By building a solid foundation and adhering to it, clients have a safety net to which they can always return.

To share information about my work, one can refer others to my website or mention my book, *Gut Driven*. The majority of my clients come from referrals or word of mouth. I encourage satisfied clients to tell friends who may be struggling to contact me. As always, I offer a free consultation before we work together, ensuring clients are comfortable and, most importantly, prepared to make changes. Sharing information is helpful, but individuals must be ready to change and committed to doing so for reasons that best suit them.

I have many parting words of wisdom to share. First, remember that you are an individual. What works for someone else may not work for you. We all want to be healthier, feel good, and live vibrant lives. However, if you change nothing, nothing will change. Committing to change is essential, and it's okay if you occasionally make mistakes – that's part of life. However, when you discover what brings you joy and maintain a balance without overindulging, positive changes occur, and progress becomes possible.

Another important aspect is knowing your body, which equips you to better advocate for yourself. Remember that you are in charge. Remember that you're paying them for their services when interacting with medical professionals. It was empowering to learn that I needed to feel comfortable with decisions made on my behalf. Thus, getting to know your body better and nourishing it with food on and off the plate—caring for body, mind, and spirit—is crucial to self-care.

The best way for someone to start working with me is to visit my website and explore what I do. I'm also on Instagram @ChefEllen. If interested, we can schedule a consultation before they commit to ensure we're a good fit. Clients must be prepared to make changes; I need them to be ready and fully committed. We can make things happen when we work together and they're dedicated. I keep clients accountable, and positive results typically follow.

About the Author

My name is Ellen Postolowski. I aim to connect with like-minded individuals and spotlight whole-body wellness. I hold a culinary degree from the Auguste Escoffier School of Culinary Arts in Boulder, Colorado, and several gut and hormonal health certifications from the Institute for Integrative Nutrition.

THE NEW ERA OF WOMEN'S HEALTH AND WELLNESS

DANIELA SCHARDINGER

As an advisor to innovators in the women's health field, I help develop strong FemTech brands and bring disruptive technology to market. As a women's health enthusiast, thought leader, and passionate FemTechie, I am dedicated to impacting and improving women's lives globally. Historically, women's health has been underrepresented in medical research and healthcare, leading to a lack of understanding and treatment options for conditions that disproportionately affect women.

It is vital to prioritize and invest in research that addresses women's health needs specifically and ensure that healthcare providers and women receive comprehensive education on women's health issues. By doing this, we can improve women's quality of care and outcomes and promote health equity for all. In addition, many women may not be aware of the full range of healthcare options available, making educational content on women's health issues, treatment options, and preventive measures crucial to building trust and credibility with the target audience.

Having specialized in this field for the past decade, my mission is to provide education and raise awareness for women's health issues, leading the charge for change. Focusing on these goals can help create a more inclusive and informed approach to women's health, ensuring that every woman has access to the care she needs and deserves.

Building a FemTech brand comes with its unique challenges. Women's health issues, such as reproductive health or uterine diseases, have been stigmatized and considered taboo in many cultures, making it difficult to address these issues openly and effectively. Furthermore, healthcare has historically been male-dominated, leading to a lack of diversity and representation in women's health brands, which can hinder connecting with a diverse group of women.

Women's health has been historically underrepresented in medical research, resulting in limited understanding and treatment options. The heavily regulated healthcare industry also adds challenges when launching a women's health brand, especially when public communication around raising awareness for specific female health issues is legally limited or even banned from social media due to taboo terminology. Women's health issues are often stigmatized, causing discomfort when discussing these topics openly. Therefore, marketing messages must be sensitive to these issues, aiming to create a safe and supportive environment for women.

It's crucial to understand the target audience and tailor messaging accordingly, as women's healthcare needs vary depending on age, life stage, health status, and other factors. Also, smaller companies innovating in this space often face competition from big pharmaceutical giants, making it difficult to stand out and differentiate a brand with limited budgets. Finally, building a women's health brand requires ethical considerations, such as ensuring patient privacy and protecting sensitive information, necessitating specific expertise and experience.

As a consultant for FemTech companies, I help bring innovation to market and build strong brands in women's health. In addition, I serve on multiple advisory boards and startup accelerators, forming part of a global network of female entrepreneurs and investors. My passion for the subject extends to participating as a speaker in international panels and conferences, solidifying my status as a thought leader in my field.

My work has led to the publication of opinion pieces in international journals and scientific articles in global medical journals focusing on women's health issues. I have been fortunate to receive support and inspiration from a powerful network of women along the way. This has led to being featured in Forbes under their SUPERWOMAN format and being named one of the top 500 FemTech personalities globally by FemTech Analytics for my work in raising awareness for women's health issues.

Over the past decade, I have specialized in women's health around the globe, building and leading companies that focus on introducing innovative medical solutions to improve women's well-being and quality of life. However, promoting women's health products has been challenging, as I have experienced firsthand. Social media bans on advertising period products and legal obstacles in raising awareness for alternatives to hormonal contraception demonstrate the difficulties in breaking taboos and stigmas around women's health issues.

Big tech companies' biases against women's issues only add to the challenge. Women's health intersect with wellness, lifestyle, and medical technology, making marketing strategies difficult to build. While it is crucial for the public to speak up about female health issues, doing so often results in censorship, criticism, or judgment. The disparity

in research and awareness is evident, with heavy menstruation affecting one in three women but receiving little attention, and erectile dysfunction research being six times more prevalent than PMS research, despite affecting fewer individuals.

Collectively addressing these issues is essential for startups and inventors to bring much-needed innovation to the market and drive adoption. My passion for this cause drives me to contribute to changing the future of how we discuss women's health issues and help innovators bring novel, less-invasive therapies and products to market successfully, ultimately improving women's lives.

I have assisted disrupters in the Fem-Tech space in winning numerous awards, including recent recognition by the World Economic Forum (WEF), which fills me with immense pride. This recognition signifies that global governments are beginning to understand the importance of better policies surrounding women's health issues. Being part of this conversation and driving change is truly exhilarating.

Advocacy for policy changes prioritizing women's health can help tackle systemic issues affecting women's healthcare. Innovators have a crucial role in advocating for policy changes that enhance access to care and address healthcare disparities, ultimately improving women's lives worldwide.

Listening to women is crucial! Women's health innovation should revolve around their needs and experiences. To develop impactful solutions and successful communication, hearing women's voices and addressing their concerns is vital.

Women have diverse healthcare needs based on age, race, ethnicity, and socio-economic status. As a result, there is a significant unmet demand for inclusive and accessible solutions for all women. Innovators in women's health have the potential to make a substantial difference in women's lives.

By prioritizing women's needs, investing in research, collaborating with healthcare professionals, embracing technology, and advocating for policy change, we can create meaningful solutions that enhance the quality of care and promote health equity for all women. I am grateful for the opportunity to play a small role in shaping the future of women's health.

I love expanding my network and helping young entrepreneurs who want to make a difference in women's lives through technology catering to women. You can reach me best through LinkedIn: linkedin.com/in/schardinger.

I believe in women supporting women. By speaking up about women's health issues, we collectively raise awareness of some of the injustices in women's health. A win for one woman is a win for all women!

About the Author

Daniela Schardinger consults FemTech Companies to bring their innovation to market and build a strong brand in women's health through her California-based boutique marketing consulting firm ELAFY Consulting LLC. She serves on multiple advisory boards and startup accelerators and has recently been featured under Forbes' SUPERWOMAN Series and named 1 of 500 FemTech Personalities globally by FemTech Analytics.

Daniela is a FemTech Enthusiast & Thought Leader driving the charge for change in Women's Health, having specialized in female healthcare around the globe for the past decade, building and leading women's health companies that focus on introducing innovative medical solutions to allow women healthier choices while improving their well-being and quality of life.

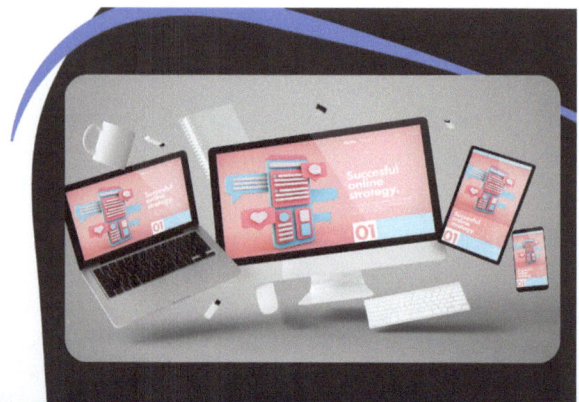

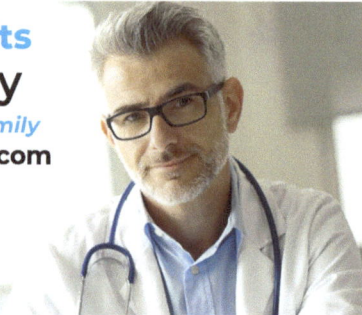

www.ingramcontent.com/pod-product-compliance
Lightning Source LLC
Chambersburg PA
CBHW041703200326
41518CB00002B/181